Buddies in the City

By Sally Cowan

Dad went with Mint to the bus stop.

It had rained overnight, and Mint got muddier and muddier on the wet road.

You will have fun with Cousin Bonny because you two are great buddies!

It was sunnier in the city.
But it was dustier than home!

Mint and Dad looked around
for Bonny.

"Mint!" cried Bonny.
"I thought you two had missed the bus!"

Dad went back home, and Mint went to Bonny's place.
She was staying for the weekend.

Mint had a wash and dried off.
She felt much fluffier!

"You will meet my buddies at a picnic!" said Bonny.

Bonny and Mint went shopping to get some snacks to take to the picnic.

At the shop, Mint spied all kinds of fruits, nuts, lollies and jellies.

Bonny handed over some coins to pay for some fruits and nuts.

"I'm going to bake a cake!"
said Bonny.
"I love to bake.
It's one of my hobbies!"

"Can I help?" asked Mint.

"That would be great!"
replied Bonny.

At the picnic, Mint tried the yummiest nuts.

And she chatted with two city bunnies.

They all had full bellies!

The next day came and it was time to go home on the bus with Dad.

Mint and Bonny cried!

"I'm the saddest chipmunk!" said Mint.

Do you like big cities, Mint?
BUS
STOP

“Yes!” Mint replied.
“But I’m happiest at home!”

CHECKING FOR MEANING

1. Who did Mint visit in the city? *(Literal)*
2. How was the city different from Mint's home? *(Literal)*
3. Do you think Mint would like to visit the city again? Why? *(Inferential)*
4. Mint and her friends had nuts and cake at their picnic. Are these good snacks for a picnic? Why? *(Evaluative)*

EXTENDING VOCABULARY

buddies	What does it mean if you are buddies with someone? What other word do you know that has a similar meaning?
sunnier	What is the base of the word *sunnier*? How has the base been changed to add the suffix? How has adding the suffix *er* changed the meaning of the base word?
happiest	How is the meaning of *happiest* different from the base word *happy*? How is the word *happy* changed when the suffix *est* is added?

MOVING BEYOND THE TEXT

1. Do you prefer the countryside or the city? Why?
2. Where are you happiest?
3. Mint and Dad took a bus to the city. What are some other ways to travel from one place to another?
4. What might you eat at a picnic? What kinds of activities might you do at a park?

TIME TO WRITE

Mint visited her cousin in the city, and they did lots of fun things. Write about a time you have visited someone or visited a new place. What did you do? What did you see?